Outlaws

by Paul Thomas

Thameside Press

Distributed in the United States by
Smart Apple Media
1980 Lookout Drive
North Mankato, MN 56003

Text copyright © Paul Thomas

ISBN 1-931983-39-9

Library of Congress Control Number 2002 141371

Printed by Midas, Hong Kong

Series editor: Veronica Ross
Editor: Honor Head
Series designer: Hayley Cove
Designer: Steve Wilson
Picture researcher: Diana Morris
Consultant: Hazel Mary Martell

Photographic credits
AKG, London: 7(bottom) Staatsbibliothek, SMPK Berlin; 42. Bridgeman Art Library: 12 Bodleian Library, Oxford;
16, 28 Private Collections. Corbis-Bettmann: 10, 19(top), 40, 41; 43(top) Dorothea Lange; 43(bottom). E.T.
Archive: 36. Mary Evans Picture Library: 9(bottom), 13(bottom), 24 Bruce Castle Collection. Ronald Grant
Archives: 5(bottom) Twentieth Century Fox. Hulton Getty Collection Ltd: 6, 11(bottom), 13(top), 21(bottom),
35(bottom). The Kobal Collection: 5(top) Twentieth Century Fox. The Mansell Collection: 15(bottom). Peter
Newark's Pictures: 4 Warner Brothers; 11(top), 14, 17(left), 17(top right), 18, 19(bottom), 20, 22, 23(top),
23(bottom), 25(top), 25(bottom), 26, 27(top), 27(bottom), 29(top), 29(bottom), 30, 31(bottom), 32, 33(top),
33(bottom), 34, 35(top), 37(top), 37(bottom), 38, 39(bottom), 40(bottom), 44(top), 44(bottom), 45(top),
45(bottom). North Wind Picture Archives: 7(top), 8, 9(top), 15(top), 21(top), 31(top), 39(top).

Words in **bold** appear in the glossary on page 46.

CONTENTS

INTRODUCTION

There are many different reasons why people throughout history have turned to a life of crime and become outlaws. For some, it was the only way they could fight injustice. For others, it was a quick way to become rich and famous.

Glamor and fame

Outlaws were usually ruthless and violent people who terrorized and threatened others. But over the years, television and films have glamorized many outlaws. Living outside the law is often seen as exciting, daring, and dangerous. Many films about Wild West outlaws, such as Jesse James and Billy the Kid, portray them as daring heroes rather than criminals.

Later, modern-day outlaws became known as gangsters. Bonnie and Clyde were two of the best-known gangsters of all time. Although they killed many people and died violently, they are characterized as a good-looking, glamorous couple in the 1967 film, starring Faye Dunaway and Warren Beatty.

Worldwide crime

In England there were different types of outlaws. During the eighteenth century, highwaymen held up people on horseback or in coaches. Perhaps the most famous highwayman is Dick Turpin.

Earlier, there were many outlaws of the seas, or pirates as they were known. The most feared and ruthless of these was Blackbeard. In Australia, outlaws were called bushrangers and were mostly escaped convicts. In his famous iron suit and helmet, Ned Kelly became the best-known outlaw from that part of the world.

Faye Dunaway and Warren Beatty in the 1967 film *Bonnie and Clyde*.

Dangerous women

Some of the most fierce and daring outlaws in history were women. Belle Starr was thought to be the toughest cowgirl in the Wild West. Mary Read and Anne Bonny were said to be two of the bravest pirates on the high seas.

Fighting for a cause

Not all outlaws chose their way of life just to become rich or for their own gain. Robin Hood in England, and William Tell in Switzerland, put themselves outside the law in order to fight injustice and not for personal gain.

Above, Henry Fonda leaping into action in the film *Jesse James* (1939).

Below, Jean Peters played *Anne of the Indies* (1951), a film about Anne Bonny, a fierce female pirate.

WILLIAM TELL

Late thirteenth century

The **legend** of William Tell is about the struggles of the people of Switzerland to overcome the harsh rule of the Austrians. Tell's bravery and courage inspired others to fight for their freedom.

William Tell was born into a **peasant** family in the **canton** of Uri. At the time of his birth, Switzerland was made up of a group of individual cantons, or communities. Along with the cantons of Schwyz (from which the name Switzerland comes) and Unterwalden, Uri was one of the main areas of peasant **resistance** against the hated and cruel Austrians.

Austrian rule

In 1273 Rudolf of Hapsburg became ruler of Germany and Switzerland. The Swiss agreed to accept his rule because he respected their laws. After Rudolf's death in 1291, his grandson, Albert of Austria, took over. Albert sent **governors** to Switzerland to make sure the Swiss people obeyed Austrian rule.

These governors were often greedy and ruthless. They demanded that the peasants hand over their cattle and other property to them, and they forced the people to pay high taxes.

William Tell symbolized Switzerland's struggle for political freedom. He is also well known for his skill with a crossbow.

Gessler's cap

In 1307 Gessler, the brutal Austrian governor of Uri, ordered the townspeople to bow to a cap hung in the square at Altdorf, as a sign of respect for the Austrian emperor. Tell refused to bow to the cap. Gessler, who had heard that Tell was an expert with the crossbow, demanded an unusual and cruel punishment.

Shooting the apple

An apple was placed on the head of William Tell's son, and Tell was ordered to shoot it off with an arrow fired from his crossbow. William Tell drew two arrows from his quiver. The little boy was so far away that the apple was almost invisible, but Tell successfully shot the apple in two without harming his son. Gessler asked Tell why he had drawn two arrows from his quiver. William Tell replied that if he had killed his son, he would have killed Gessler.

William Tell was ordered to shoot an apple off his son's head. His son was so far away, it was likely he would miss the apple and kill his son.

Switzerland

Switzerland is best known for its range of high mountains called the Swiss Alps and its picture-book beauty. It is also known as a peaceful country that has not been involved in a war since 1815. It stayed neutral during the two World Wars earlier this century. Many international organizations, such as the **Red Cross**, are based in Switzerland.

A great storm

Gessler called William Tell a **traitor** and an **assassin**, and ordered his arrest. Tell was captured and taken on board a boat sailing for Gessler's **fortress**, where there was a prison. But as they crossed the great lake, a violent storm arose, and the boat was unable to pull into the shore. Gessler was terrified of drowning, so he agreed to free Tell, who was known for his sailing skills. Tell said he would bring the boat safely to shore. But he tricked the crew and leaped overboard with his crossbow.

Death of Gessler

Tell was so afraid that Gessler would capture and torture his family that he vowed to kill him. He did not have to wait long for an opportunity to carry out his promise. Gessler and his crew survived the storm. As they were making their way to the fortress, they were ambushed by Tell, who shot Gessler with his crossbow.

William Tell escaped from Gessler's boat by leaping ashore during a storm.

Liberation of Switzerland

Tell escaped and returned to Uri, where he organized the Swiss rebels into a powerful fighting force. His aim was to drive the Austrians out of Switzerland. In 1315 the Swiss rebels faced the Austrian Army at the Battle of Morganten. The Austrians were better equipped, but the Swiss put up a fierce fight and won. This battle has become one of the most important in Swiss history.

The crossbow

William Tell was renown for his skill with the crossbow. It was originally a **medieval** weapon that could fire small arrows with great force. A crossbow was usually made of a metal bow that was attached to the end of a wooden handle. There was a groove inside the handle that held the arrow, a trigger to release it, and a crank for drawing the bowstring tight.

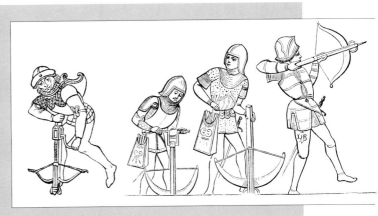

A free country

The victory at Morganten encouraged other cantons such as Lucerne, Zurich, and Berne to join the rebellion. Eventually the cantons joined together to create a **confederation** and became known as The Confederation of Switzerland, an independent and free country.

Man, or myth?

Nothing is known about William Tell after the Battle of Morganten, although some books say he died in a flood, in 1350. Many people believe that he is just a popular legend. But for the Swiss people, William Tell is a national hero who symbolizes their struggle for freedom.

The Swiss defeating the Austrians at the Battle of Morganten.

ROBIN HOOD

Early fourteenth century

The most famous outlaw of all time is Robin Hood, and yet he is also the one we know the least about. We do not even know if he really existed, or if he is just a mythical figure whose story has grown over the centuries.

The story of Robin Hood's life was passed down from one generation to another through songs and tales, so it is difficult to know how much of the legend is true. Some believe that the adventures of Robin Hood are based on stories of lots of different outlaws mixed up together. One story claims that Robin lived in Sherwood Forest, in Nottinghamshire, in the twelfth century. Another story says that Robin Hood was the Earl of Huntingdon, Robert Fitzooth, who was outlawed for his part in a rebellion in 1265.

The real Robin Hood?

Records show that a person named Robert Hood was born in 1290, in Wakefield, Yorkshire. He may have been the famous outlaw because at that time Robin was a popular nickname for people named Robert. In the legend, Robin Hood married Maid Marian. Records show that Robert Hood's wife was called Matilda, which could have become Marian.

Even though little is known about him, Robin Hood is the most famous outlaw of all time.

Rebel and outlaw

In 1322 Robin's landlord, the Earl of Lancaster, ordered his **tenants** to rebel against King Edward II. A tenant had to obey, and Robin followed the Earl into battle as an archer. The revolt was soon crushed, and Lancaster was tried for treason and beheaded.

Robin Hood and his men robbing the Bishop of Hereford, who has been tied to a tree.

Band of Merry Men

Robin's followers are as much a part of the legend as Robin Hood himself. Little John, who was given his nickname as a joke because he was so big and strong, was one of the first members of Robin Hood's band of outlaws. Friar Tuck, shown here on the donkey, is another well-known member of the band. He was a jolly monk who enjoyed his food and good company.

Escape to the forest

All of the Earl's possessions were taken by the king, and his followers were outlawed. Robin could not return home, so he fled into Barnsdale Forest, in Yorkshire, which was joined to Nottinghamshire's Sherwood Forest. The two forests covered a huge area of land and made an ideal hiding place.

A legend is born

A road ran through the forests joining London with the North. Robbers made rich pickings from the travelers who used it. And Robin Hood was no exception. According to legend, Robin Hood robbed the rich to give to the poor. Tales of how he could outwit the king's men and humiliate the wealthy and influential made him very popular with the poor. His skill as an archer and stories about his faithful band of followers soon became part of the legend.

A private hunting ground

The forest then would have been very different from the forest we know today. It was the private hunting ground of the lords of the manor or the king, and it contained lots of game, including deer. Much of the forest would have been densely wooded, but there would also have been clearings where Robin and his men could set up camp.

The king's plan

In 1323 King Edward II traveled to the north of England to make sure the rebellion of the previous year was over and to capture Robin Hood. He planned to disguise himself and his knights as monks and ride into Sherwood Forest, in the hope that Robin and his men would try to rob him.

A royal pardon

The plan worked, and the king and his men were stopped by the outlaws who demanded money. The king said he had £40, so Robin took half and gave the rest back. Edward then produced the royal **seal** on his finger. The outlaws knelt down in front of the seal and swore their **allegiance** to the king. Edward said he would **pardon** all of the outlaws if they agreed to come to his court and serve him. They all agreed.

Records show Robin Hood's name in the household accounts of Edward II in 1324, but after that his name vanishes. It was said that he could not settle down and serve the king, so he returned to the forest.

King Edward II, who pardoned Robin Hood and his men, ruled England for twenty years with his wife, Queen Isabella of France.

Rob Roy

Rob Roy Macgregor, the "Robin Hood" of Scotland, spent his life in the Scottish Highlands. He was an excellent swordsman and had a reputation for being fearless. In 1691 he joined the **Jacobites**, who were supporters of the **exiled** king, James II. The Jacobite rising failed in 1716, and Rob became an outlaw. His reputation as a hero of the people spread across Scotland. He was captured and jailed in Newgate Prison, in London, in 1722, but he was pardoned in 1727. He died seven years later. His fame grew when Sir Walter Scott's novel, *Rob Roy*, was published in 1818.

Deathbed shot

Robin's adventures in the forests continued until 1346, when he is thought to have died at Kirklees **Priory**, near Leeds, after a long illness. Legend says that on his deathbed, he shot an arrow from the window of his room. Robin Hood asked to be buried wherever the arrow fell.

The spot said to be his grave can still be seen near the priory. Many stories and songs about Robin Hood have been handed down from generation to generation and have helped turn him into the legend we know today. One of these is the story *Ivanhoe*, by Sir Walter Scott.

Robin Hood shot his last arrow when he was dying. He was buried at the spot where the arrow landed.

BLACKBEARD

1680–1718

Many sailors turned to piracy at the end of the war of the **Spanish Succession**. Among these was one of the most feared and hated pirates of all time, Blackbeard.

Mystery surrounds the beginning of Blackbeard's life. It is not certain whether he was born in Bristol, England, or in Jamaica, in about 1680. Even the spelling of his real name is unclear – it could have been Edward Teach, Tatch, or Thatch. Blackbeard went to the West Indies in 1701 to fight for England as a **privateer**, but he soon turned to piracy.

In 1713 Blackbeard captured a French merchant ship. He armed the ship with forty large cannons and renamed it *Queen Anne's Revenge*.

Demon of the seas

Teach was nicknamed Blackbeard because of his appearance, which struck terror into his victims. His thick, black beard was long and braided and tied with ribbons. He was well over 6 feet (1.8 m) tall, and when he fought, he would wear a sling over his shoulders with six pistols tucked into it. Blackbeard would swoop down on his victims with a wild and fierce look in his eyes.

When he went into battle, Blackbeard would light slow-burning fuses under his hat. Black smoke curled around his head, making him look like a demon.

A pirate's life

Most pirates were desperate robbers and killers on the run from the law. Some were honest seamen, who were forced into piracy when their ships were captured. The pirate captain was elected by the crew, but he had command only when the ship was about to attack. After that, every man could do as he pleased. **Plunder** was divided fairly among the crew, and if a pirate suffered an injury during a fight, he was given extra payment. Pirates drank huge amounts of alcohol, and a mixture of rum and gunpowder was a favorite cocktail. Most pirates died either fighting or on the **gallows**.

Shipwrecked!

Blackbeard and his crew then decided to sail farther north to Topsail Inlet, in North Carolina. It was here that two of his ships, including *Queen Anne's Revenge*, were wrecked. Some of his crew left to join other pirate ships, but Blackbeard and about thirty men decided to approach the king of England, George I, and beg for mercy.

The coast of America

By 1717 Blackbeard's fearsome reputation was established. With his crew of ruthless pirates, he sailed through the West Indies, and north along the American coast, capturing and plundering many ships. In 1718 Blackbeard **blockaded** Charleston Harbor, in South Carolina. He sent some of his men into the town to demand a chest full of gold and jewels. The residents knew that Blackbeard would attack if they didn't pay up.

A drawing of an English privateer ship capturing a **frigate**. Many privateers, such as Blackbeard, became pirates.

Blackbeard raided ships sailing along the American coast. He was ruthless and fought fiercely.

Secret plans

The pirates wanted a royal pardon, which meant they would not be hanged. But Blackbeard had his own secret plan. He had already set up a business partnership with the governor of North Carolina, Charles Eden. Blackbeard agreed to share his booty with Eden in exchange for a royal pardon. This was easy for the governor to arrange, and Blackbeard walked away a free man, while his crew members were hanged in Virginia.

But Blackbeard soon became bored with his law-abiding life, and he began to run out of money. It was not long before he gave up life on dry land and went back to piracy.

The people seek revenge

Blackbeard continued robbing ships and demanding money from the people of North Carolina. He also blocked the rivers and demanded money from any vessels that used them.

Eventually the local people decided that they had to do something about Blackbeard. They knew they could not go to Eden, their own governor. Instead, they went to the governor of the neighboring state of Virginia, Alexander Spotswood. He wanted to protect Virginia's trade from the pirates.

Help at last

Spotswood planned to ambush Blackbeard's ships and hired Captain Robert Maynard to hunt him down. On November 22, 1718, Captain Maynard set sail with two ships, **HMS** *Pearl* and HMS *Lyme*, in search of Blackbeard. They caught up with his ship in the Ocracoke Inlet, off the coast of North Carolina.

When Blackbeard was finally killed, his head was cut off and hung from the bow of his ship to prove to people that he was really dead.

The pirate flags

Many pirates sailed under a black flag with a white skull and crossbones on it. This was called the Jolly Roger. Some pirates made up their own version of the Jolly Roger. Blackbeard's flag had a black background, with the picture of a white skeleton holding an hourglass in one hand and an arrow striking at a bleeding heart in the other. These pictures warned his victims that their time was running out.

The last fight

As they came alongside the pirate vessel, Maynard's ships hoisted the **king's flag**. Blackbeard fired his cannons at them. Maynard's ships did not have any big guns, but they fired back with small firearms. The pirate ship ran aground, and sailors and pirates boarded each other's ships to fight.

Maynard and Blackbeard fought each other face-to-face, with pistols and swords. Blackbeard was shot five times with a pistol and received twenty **cutlass** wounds before he fell to the deck, dead.

The other pirates fought on, until only six of them remained alive, all wounded. Maynard cut off Blackbeard's head and hung it from a bar over the **bow** of his ship. Legend has it that the headless corpse swam around the ship three times before sinking.

MARY READ

1690–1720

Disguised as a man, Mary Read roamed the seas as a fierce and bloody pirate. She could use a sword and a pistol as well as any male pirate.

Mary Read was born in England, in 1690. Her father was a sea captain who left his family soon after Mary was born. Read's mother raised her daughter as a boy. Some say this was because she wanted an inheritance from her wealthy mother-in-law, who would be more likely to leave money to a boy. Others say it was because she had been deeply affected by the earlier death of her baby son.

In search of adventure

When her grandmother died, Read continued to dress as a boy. When she was 13, she was sent to work for a French lady as a **footboy**. But Read was outgoing and restless and eager for some excitement in her life. She soon became bored with domestic service and decided to go in search of adventure.

She signed up to work on board a warship as a powder monkey. Powder monkeys were boys who made sure the **ammunition** or gunpowder for the big cannons was always ready. No one guessed that she was really a girl in disguise.

Mary Read is one of the most famous female pirates in history. She dressed like a man and fought as hard as any of the male pirates.

Mary Read was disguised as a man when her pirate ship was captured by another. She was taken prisoner because she was the only English "man" on board.

A short marriage

Read stayed on board the warship for six years, until she deserted. She joined a **foot regiment** in Flanders (Belgium) and went to fight the French. It was during this time that she fell in love with one of the officers. Read took a great risk and revealed her true identity to him. Before long the couple were married. They left the army to open a tavern near Breda, in the Netherlands.

In disguise again

Read's husband died suddenly, and the tavern started to lose money. To avoid a life of poverty, Read once again disguised herself as a man and joined another foot regiment. But she soon deserted the regiment for a ship bound for the West Indies. Read's ship was captured by English pirates and, as the only English "man" on board, they took her with them. She stayed with the pirates until 1717, when George I of England issued a pardon for any pirates who would leave the trade.

Anne Bonny

Anne Bonny, shown here (left) with Mary Read, was born in Ireland in 1700 and raised in Charleston, South Carolina. She became a pirate when she met her pirate-husband, James Bonny. Several years later she ran off with the pirate Calico Jack. They sailed the seas off Cuba and Haiti, attacking Spanish ships. After her trial and release, Bonny returned to Charleston.

Life on land

Read took advantage of the offer of a pardon and returned to life on land. But she was soon back in disguise and went to join an outfit of privateers who were preying on Spanish ships. In 1718 Read's ship was captured by a pirate ship commanded by Captain Jack Rackham, known as Calico Jack.

Read and Bonny

With Calico Jack was his companion, Anne Bonny, who was also disguised as a man. Mary Read and Anne Bonny became close friends, and Read confessed to Bonny that she was a woman. Soon after this, Read fell in love with Peter Hines, an Englishman who was serving on board. Hines was not a good swordsman, but Read's love for him was so strong that she arranged to take Hines's place in a duel, and she fought it successfully for him.

Too drunk to fight

In 1720 Captain Rackham's ship was captured off the coast of Jamaica, by a government ship. Rackham and his men had been drinking so heavily that they were too drunk to fight. The men remained below deck, still drinking, while Read and Bonny, armed with swords and pistols, tried to fight off the government men.

Mary Read fought a duel on behalf of her lover, Peter Hines. Read was a much better swordsman than Hines and had a greater chance of winning.

The pirate queen

Ching Yi Saoa sailed the China Seas at the beginning of the nineteenth century. She ran a fleet of nearly 2,000 junks, or Chinese ships (right), crewed by over 70,000 male and female pirates. She made a fortune by plundering merchant ships, raiding towns, and taking hundreds of prisoners for ransom. The Chinese government tried to capture her many times, but they always failed. They eventually offered her a pardon, which she accepted, and settled down to a life of luxury.

Mary Read visited Calico Jack Rackham in prison in Jamaica, before he was hanged for piracy. Read was freed because she was pregnant.

Capture and trial

Read and Bonny put up a fierce fight, but they were soon disarmed. They were arrested, together with Rackham and the rest of the crew, and sent to be tried for piracy. They were taken to St. Jago de la Vega, in Jamaica. Jack Rackham and several of his crew were found guilty and sentenced to death by hanging. This was the usual punishment for acts of piracy.

Witnesses were called who said Read had taken part in acts of piracy around Jamaica. They also said that she wore men's clothes and was able to use a pistol and a sword as well as any man.

Death, or prison?

Read and Bonny were both found guilty of piracy but claimed they were pregnant by saying, "My lord, we plead our bellies." They were examined and were not given the death penalty because they were due to give birth. Read was not to enjoy her reprieve for long, however. Just a few months later, she died of a fever.

DICK TURPIN

1705–1739

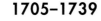

Highway robbery thrived in Great Britain during the seventeenth and eighteenth centuries, when roads were deserted, coach travel slow, and the law weak. There were many highwaymen but none as famous as Dick Turpin.

Turpin was born on September 25, 1705, at the Ben Inn, in the village of Hempstead, Essex. The inn was owned by his father, who was an ex-butcher. At the age of 16, Turpin became an apprentice to a London butcher. The move to the big city gave him a taste for the richer things in life, which he was unable to afford as a butcher. So at night Turpin started a second career as a footpad, a highwayman, or robber, on foot. This made him enough money to be able to return to Essex, get married, and set up his own butcher's shop.

The Essex Gang

But the business was not very successful, and Dick Turpin soon returned to a life of crime to pay for his extravagant lifestyle. He joined a notorious gang of burglars, known as the Essex Gang. The members of the gang were among the most wanted men in the London area.

Legend says that Dick Turpin rode from London to York to escape capture, in just 12 hours. His horse, Black Bess, died of exhaustion just before they reached York.

Dick Turpin shooting the keeper who discovered his hideout in Epping Forest. After this a reward was offered for Turpin's capture.

Through the window

The gang poached deer and broke into houses, threatening and torturing the people who lived there before escaping with whatever they could. A £100 reward was offered for their capture. The authorities eventually caught up with the gang, but Turpin escaped by jumping out of a window. Two other members of the gang were arrested, tried, and hanged.

Dog eat dog

Turpin decided to return to highway robbery, but this time on horseback. He set up his hideout in a cave in Epping Forest. In 1736 Turpin attempted to rob a smartly dressed rider on the Cambridge Road. His intended victim burst into laughter and cried, "What! Dog eat dog?" The other man was Tom King, one of the most famous highwaymen of the day who was known as the gentleman highwayman. Turpin and King became partners. King taught Turpin that he would be more successful if he treated his victims with a little courtesy.

Tyburn gallows

Tyburn gallows, also known as the Tyburn Tree, was the main place of execution by hanging from 1300 to 1783. It was near London's Marble Arch, and a plaque marks the spot. A hanging was a popular social event. High prices were paid for the best seats at the gallows. The prisoner was taken to the gallows on the back of a horse-drawn cart. This journey was like a royal procession, with the crowds cheering and throwing flowers at the prisoner.

Dick Turpin may have shot his partner, Tom King, while trying to keep him from being arrested.

Fatal chase

The partnership only lasted a year. Turpin and King had stolen a famous racehorse called White Stockings, which was easily recognized by many people. One evening Turpin was seen riding through the streets of London on the horse. He was reported, and the authorities set up a chase. As they raced after him, Turpin saw King being arrested and went to help him. In the chaos that followed, King was shot dead. Some say he was shot by the authorities, other reports say that he was accidentally shot by Turpin, who then managed to escape.

A new identity

Dick Turpin moved north and set himself up in Yorkshire, as a country gentleman named John Palmer. Turpin made money by stealing sheep and horses. In 1739, after a particularly wild night, he began firing off his pistols in the street. Annoyed neighbors reported him, and he ended up in jail, while the local authorities investigated his recent activities.

Highwaymen

Many highwaymen adopted amusing disguises when robbing travelers. James Collet disguised himself as a bishop, while Thomas Sympson wore women's clothes. One highwayman, Jonathan Simpson, wore ice skates and held up people on the frozen Thames River. But the popular image of a highwayman is of a man on horseback, pointing a pistol, wearing a black eye mask and cloak, and making the command, "Stand and deliver. Your money, or your life."

All is revealed

Under the **alias** John Palmer, Turpin wrote to his family asking them to come forward to help him clear his name. Unfortunately for Turpin, the postmaster was his old schoolteacher who had taught him to read and write. Amazingly, after so many years, the teacher recognized his pupil's handwriting and reported his discovery of the letter to the authorities.

Going in style

John Palmer was identified as Dick Turpin and arrested. He admitted everything, was tried at York, and sentenced to be hanged. On the morning of April 7, 1739, Turpin was taken to the gallows on what is now York racecourse. He bowed and waved to all the spectators who had come to see England's most famous highwayman die. Legend has it that when he arrived at the gallows, he chatted in a friendly manner with the hangman. He then stood with his head high, the noose around his neck, and hurled himself from the scaffold to ensure a quick death.

Illustration for Alfred Noyes's poem *The Ballad of Dick Turpin,* showing him wearing a typical highwayman's hat and mask.

BELLE STARR

1846–1889

Belle Starr was a well-educated, intelligent woman who rode horseback dressed in velvet and feathers. She was also one of the most fierce and reckless outlaws in the western United States.

Belle Starr was born Myra Belle Shirley, on February 5, 1846, in Missouri. Belle came from a wealthy family. Her father, John Shirley, was a businessman from Virginia who bought a **homestead** in Missouri, to make a new life for himself and his family.

Bad company

When she was eight, Starr went to Carthage Female Academy, which was one of the finest schools in the area. This peaceful life continued until a local war broke out on the borders of Kansas and Missouri, and gangs set fire to John Shirley's ranch. He decided to move his family away from the trouble, and they left for Texas. Belle Starr was 15 years old.

The family settled in a small town called Scyene, east of Dallas. By the time Belle was 18, it was obvious to most people who knew her that she preferred the company of gangsters and thieves.

Belle Starr was nicknamed the Bandit Queen of Oklahoma. She joined many other outlaws and ran a hideout for wanted criminals.

Encountering Outlaws

Belle's first encounter with outlaws was with the handsome Cole Younger, who was part of the Jesse James Gang. She sheltered Younger when he was on the run after robbing a bank. They had a child, Pearl, but Cole Younger abandoned Starr and their daughter.

Belle met another outlaw, Jim Reed, and they soon set up a partnership. They moved to California, where their son was born, but returned to Texas, in 1869. They made a living **rustling** horses and robbing banks and trains.

Bandit Queen

Belle called herself the Bandit Queen. She always insisted on riding sidesaddle, and she wore velvet dresses and feathers, as well as a holster with pistols. When Jim Reed was killed in 1874, Starr decided to leave her children with her mother and rode out of town seeking adventure and a new partner.

Women outlaws

Belle Starr was not the only female outlaw in the American West. Cattle Annie McDougal (above left) and Little Britches (Jennie) Metcalf (above right), started their careers by **bootlegging** whiskey before switching to rustling cattle. Rose Dunn, nicknamed the Rose of Cimarron, became one of the best horse thieves in the West.

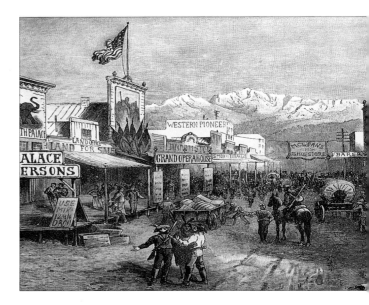

An illustration of a Wild West town, as it would have been in Belle Starr's time. It shows familiar sights, such as an opera house and a grocery store.

Hideout ranch

In 1880 Belle married a **Native American**, a tall, slim Cherokee named Sam Starr. They led a gang that stole cattle and horses. Their home was a log cabin near Fort Smith, in Arkansas, which became well known as a hideout for some of the most wanted outlaws of the day. Belle was thought to be the mastermind behind the gang's activities.

Law expert

Belle Starr and her gang were charged many times with horse-stealing and other criminal acts. But unlike most of her fellow outlaws, Starr was educated, and she understood the law. She was smart enough to get many of the cases against her dismissed due to lack of evidence. In 1883 both Belle and Sam Starr were convicted of stealing horses and imprisoned. But as soon as they were released from jail, they went back to their life of crime.

Cowgirls and the rodeo

Many women in the American West learned the same skills as cowboys. Cowgirls doing trick-riding, roping, and bronco-riding became very popular at rodeo shows. One of the best-known cowgirls was Lucille Mulhall. She could catch eight horses at a time with one throw of her lasso. Calamity Jane (right) joined Buffalo Bill's Wild West show and demonstrated her riding and sharpshooting skills. Annie Oakley was another top attraction in Buffalo Bill's show. She could shoot a cigarette from her husband's lips, dimes from his fingers, and hit a target behind her using a hand mirror.

This painting, called *Rustlers,* by William H. D. Koerner, shows outlaws riding in to steal cattle and horses. Starr and her partners were expert cattle rustlers.

The unknown killer

Belle told Jim that the authorities had no case against him and that he should give himself up and plead not guilty. She planned to handle his case in court. On February 3, 1889, Belle Starr and Jim July set out for Fort Smith. The following morning Jim was seen going on alone. Later, Belle was found dying in the dust, having been shot in the back.

The identity of Belle Starr's killer has never been discovered. Some people said the murderer was Jim July because Starr had decided not to help him. It was even thought it could have been her son, Edward, with whom she had a stormy relationship, but the truth will never be known.

Belle Starr photographed with one of her many outlaw partners, a Native American named Blue Duck.

A price on her head

The Starrs were now so notorious that the United States government offered $10,000 in gold coins for information leading to their arrest. Although this was a huge amount of money in those days, no one came forward with evidence that could be used to prosecute the pair.

A new partner

Sam Starr was killed in a gunfight with a deputy-sheriff in 1886. Belle mourned his death, but she soon took up with another outlaw. Like Sam, Jim July was a Native American, a Creek Indian. They met when Jim, who was wanted for robbery, was hiding out at Starr's cabin.

JESSE JAMES

1847–1882

Jesse James came from a respectable, religious family. He grew up during the **Civil War** and the railroad boom, both of which affected his life greatly.

James's father was a Baptist preacher who set up a Baptist school in Clay County, Missouri, where James was born. He had a brother, Frank, and a sister, Susan. When Jesse was only three years old, his father left for California to try and find gold. He was only there for a few weeks before he died of an unknown illness.

Guerrilla gangs

James's mother remarried a wealthy man and had four more children. The family were slaveowners, and when the Civil War began in 1861, they sided with the South. The southern states supported slavery, while the northern states wanted to see slavery abolished.

In the summer of 1863, when Jesse was 16, his family was attacked by antislavery supporters. His stepfather was nearly hanged, and Jesse was badly beaten. As a result, Jesse joined a **guerrilla** group fighting against the North. He learned how to fight and how to shoot.

A photograph of Jesse James, age 17, taken during the Civil War.

The great gold rush

There have been many gold rushes in American history, but the most famous was in 1849, when gold was discovered at Sutter's Mill on the American River, in California. It caused the largest migration of people over the longest distances in the briefest span of time in the history of the world. California's population grew from 14,000 in 1848 to 380,000 in 1860. People even came from such places as China, Australia, and Europe.

End of the war

Two years later, the Civil War ended. Jesse and his brother, Frank, who had also fought in the Civil War, found it difficult to settle into a routine life after the excitement of the war years. They met up with some other ex-guerrillas, including Jim and Cole Younger, who were also bored with the peace and with the thought of a lifetime spent as farmers.

The James-Younger Gang

The Younger brothers and the James brothers decided to escape from everyday life and to look for excitement outside the law. Together they formed a ruthless gang led by Jesse James. Over the next 16 years, the gang brutally robbed banks and trains, killing many innocent staff and bystanders.

Jesse James and his brother, Frank, photographed with the Younger brothers. Together they formed one of the most violent and ruthless gangs in the American West.

Cole Younger

Bob Younger (rear)

Jesse James

Frank James

Train robbers

Railroad building had boomed in the United States since the Civil War. Railroads stretched across the country, carrying valuable cargo, such as gold and money, as well as passengers. Many gangs had already begun to realize that trains were a good source of loot, and the James Gang was no exception. They carried out a daring train robbery in their home state of Missouri, at Gad's Hill. They also continued to rob banks, escaping with large sums of money.

Pinkerton detectives

In 1871 banking officials hired the Pinkerton National Detective Agency to try and capture Jesse James. A Pinkerton agent was killed when sent out to arrest the James brothers. Four years later a bomb was thrown into their mother's house, causing her to lose an arm, and killing their stepbrother. It was believed to have been thrown by Pinkerton men. Public sympathy turned in Jesse's favor, and the detectives were called off.

Robin Hood of the West

The gang had many supporters among ordinary people who disliked the banks. This was because banks charged high interest rates on borrowed money. Jesse's supporters were very pleased to see the banks and railroads robbed of their profits, and Jesse James gained a reputation as a modern-day Robin Hood. Dime novels and boys' comics all made up stories about Jesse James and his exciting adventures.

Legend says that Jesse would steal only from passengers from the northern states when he robbed trains. He said the northerners had forced him into a life of crime, so only northerners should pay. But in reality it was mainly southerners who were terrorized and killed by his gang.

This illustration from *The Police Gazette* shows Jesse James and his gang robbing a train in 1881. They stole cargo and forced passengers to hand over their valuables.

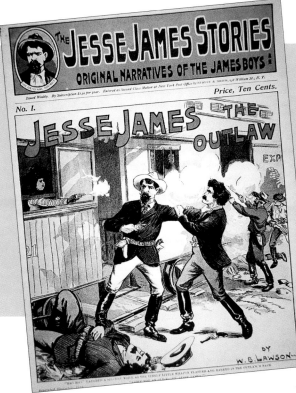

Dime novels

During Jesse James's life and after he was killed, his adventures were written about in many books, such as *The Jesse James Stories*. These were called "dime novels" because they only cost a dime, or ten cents. They were the idea of Erastus Beadle, who launched the series in June 1860. Dime novels brought the excitement of the West to readers all over America. Robert Leroy Parker was one person who enjoyed dime novels. He was later known as Butch Cassidy.

Robert Ford, a new member of Jesse's gang, shot him in the back of the head.

Jesse betrayed

In 1881 Jesse robbed a train in Missouri, killing the conductor and a passenger. This caused public outrage and led to a reward of $10,000 for his capture, dead or alive. Some time later, two new gang members, Charles and Robert Ford, were staying with Jesse prior to a bank robbery planned for the next day. After finishing his breakfast, Jesse reached up to straighten a picture. Robert Ford pulled out his gun, aimed it at Jesse, and shot him in the back of the head. He later claimed the reward.

Jesse's brother, Frank, gave himself up in exchange for being pardoned for most of his crimes. He served two years in prison and was released in 1885. Frank was to live for another 30 years as a law-abiding farmer, until his death in 1915.

NED KELLY

1855–1880

In Australia outlaws were called bushrangers because they hid in the vast bush. During the nineteenth century, there were many bushrangers, but the best-known was Ned Kelly.

During the nineteenth century, many criminals from England and Ireland were sent to penal colonies in Australia. Ned Kelly's father was transported to Australia from Belfast, Ireland, for stealing pigs. The Kellys decided to stay in Australia, and settled in the state of Victoria.

Ned Kelly's father died when Ned was 11 years old. This made Ned, the eldest of seven children, the head of the family. The Kellys were constantly in trouble with the police for all sorts of petty crimes, and Ned Kelly grew up believing that the authorities were the enemy.

A bad start

At the age of 15, Ned Kelly was arrested for taking part in a robbery. But there was no evidence to link him to the robbery, so he was allowed to go. Six months later he was arrested again, this time on a charge of assaulting a police officer. In 1871 he was rearrested, and he was jailed for three years.

This photograph was taken of Ned Kelly just a few days before his execution in 1880. He was captured in a spectacular shoot-out.

The Kelly Gang, with Ned holding the shotgun, and his brother, Dan, in the middle.

The Kelly Gang

In April 1878 a policeman went to the Kelly household to arrest Ned's brother, Dan. Their mother hit the policeman over the head with a spade! Although the policeman was not seriously hurt, she was sentenced to three years in prison while her sons went on the run. Ned and Dan Kelly were joined by two other outlaws and formed the Kelly Gang. In October 1878 two police search parties set out to find the Kelly Gang. They came upon the gang at Stringybark Creek and, in the gunfight that followed, three policemen were shot and killed.

Penal colonies

Penal colonies were prisons where convicts from Great Britain were sent to help ease the overcrowding in British jails. The convicts were transported in special ships, like the one shown here. The first penal colony was set up in what is now the city of Sydney, by Captain Arthur Phillip, who landed in Australia on January 26, 1788. Convicts were poorly housed, clothed, and fed. They often worked in chain gangs and were severely punished for the smallest offense. In the 1800s **immigrants** began to set up farms in Australia, and convicts were used as farmworkers.

Showing off

The people of the state of Victoria were shocked at the news. A reward of $600 was offered for Kelly's arrest, and an army of police scoured the bush to try to find him. But instead of lying low, the Kelly Gang seemed to be making fun of the police. On December 9, 1878, the Kelly Gang robbed a bank in Euroa, Victoria. Instead of making a quick escape, Kelly insisted on taking the bewildered bank manager, his family, and two servants on a picnic where he showed off his riding skills. The police did not catch them. It seemed the Kelly Gang was always one step ahead.

Ned Kelly's suit of armor

Ned Kelly's armor was made out of plowshares, the metal blades on a plow that turn the soil. They were melted and shaped to fit. The suit consisted of four pieces: a massive square helmet with a slit for the eyes, a front part that covered his chest and stomach, and a back piece and an apron that covered his thighs. His arms and legs were left unprotected. The suit weighed nearly 110 pounds (50 kg).

The Kelly Gang holding up the police station at the town of Jerilderie.

The master plan

In June 1880, Kelly devised his criminal master plan. He intended to lure a trainload of policemen into an **ambush** and topple the train into a deep gully, killing all the police. With all the district's police dead, Kelly planned to rob all the banks in the area.

Ned and his gang planned to wear suits of armor made from plowshares. But his scheme did not go according to plan. The police were warned, escaped the ambush unhurt, and surrounded the hotel where the Kelly Gang was waiting. A fierce gunfight followed.

The final fight

Each member of the Kelly Gang was hit by gunfire. Ned, although wounded, approached the police wearing his armor and firing his guns. Most of the police bullets bounced off the thick armor, but one policeman fired at Ned's unprotected legs, and he fell to the ground.

Ned Kelly was charged with murder, found guilty, and sentenced to death. He was hanged in Melbourne, on November 11, 1880. His last words were, "Such is life."

In disguise

On another occasion in the town of Jerilderie, the Kellys locked the police in their cells, put on their uniforms, and made one officer introduce them around the town as the new police force. The next day they robbed the bank.

Ned Kelly was eventually captured, tried, and sentenced to death. A petition of 60,000 signatures did not even save his life.

BILLY THE KID

1859–1881

Patrick Henry McCarty also called himself William Bonney and Kid Antrim. But at the time of his death, he was known as Billy the Kid, one of the most feared outlaws in the American West.

The Kid was born in November 1859, on New York's East Side. The family moved to Kansas when Billy was a child, and his father died there. He then moved with his mother and brother to Colorado, where his mother married William H. Antrim. The family moved to Silver City, New Mexico. Billy the Kid was an expert card-player by the age of eight, and, when he was 12 years old, it is said that he killed a man with a knife for insulting his mother. By the time he was 18 years old, Billy the Kid had been charged with 12 murders.

Cowboy Kid

The Kid became known as an expert who could escape from any jail. The Kid's first escape from jail was when he was 15 years old. He was locked up for stealing laundry, but he escaped by climbing up the chimney. He stole a horse and headed for Arizona, hoping to become a cowboy. For the next two years, the Kid worked on many sheep and cattle ranches, learning the skills of a professional cowboy.

Billy the Kid started his life of crime when still a child. He became a ruthless gunslinger.

First victim

The Kid also learned how to use a pistol and a rifle. In 1877, at the age of 17, he became involved in a fight with the local blacksmith. The Kid drew his gun and shot the man, who died the next day. The Kid was charged with murder and put in jail, but he managed to escape and fled to Lincoln County, New Mexico.

A major dispute

The Kid took a job on a ranch owned by an Englishman named John Tunstall. A very strong friendship grew between the Kid and Tunstall that was to be the downfall of the Kid. A major dispute had been growing between Tunstall and another local rancher, who had falsely accused Tunstall of cheating. The authorities took the side of the local rancher against the Englishman.

Cowboys

Two important events in the year for cowboys were the massive cattle roundups every spring and fall. Cowboys would **brand** newborn calves and choose cattle to take to the market. Then they began the long drive to a railroad for the cattle to be shipped east. On the trail cowboys faced many dangers, including wild animals, rustlers (cattle thieves), and stampedes.

The Kid became a cowboy when he left home, working on sheep and cattle ranches.

Theft and shootings became a way of life for
Billy the Kid when he was on the run from the law.

New Mexico

By now Billy the Kid was on the run and
leading a life of stealing cattle and general
lawlessness. Pat Garrett, who had been an
outlaw and a friend of the Kid's, was elected
sheriff with the task of finding Billy the Kid.
His posse eventually tracked down the Kid
and his gang at a house in New Mexico.

Pat Garrett, a former friend of the Kid's,
was given the job of
capturing him.

Meaningless death

Tunstall heard that the sheriff and a **posse**
were coming after him. Rather than have a
gunfight with the local deputy, Tunstall left
the ranch with the Kid and his other men.
But the deputy and his posse rode after
Tunstall, stopped him, and shot him dead.
The Kid, with the other men from the
ranch, looked on helplessly. Billy vowed
to avenge Tunstall's death. The next month,
the Kid's gang caught up with two of
Tunstall's killers on their way to prison
with a deputy. The Kid shot them dead
and killed the deputy. A few weeks later
he shot two more of Tunstall's killers.

Gunfight at the OK Corral

Wyatt Earp (1848–1929) was one of the best-known sheriffs and gunfighters of the American West. He gained his reputation at the famous gunfight at the OK Corral, Tombstone, Arizona, on October 26, 1881. The three Earp brothers and Wyatt's friend, Doc Holliday, shot dead three members of the Clanton Gang in a short but ferocious gunfight. Wyatt Earp was the only one not to be injured.

Starved out of hiding

Garrett's men surrounded the house, making escape impossible. After a few days, when the food and water had run out, Pat Garrett had an idea. He got his men to light a fire and fry food within smelling distance of the house. After a little while, the hungry outlaws surrendered. The Kid was imprisoned and in 1881 stood trial accused of three murders.

Final escape

The Kid was found guilty and sentenced to hang. But he managed to escape with the help of a friend who left a gun in an outhouse for him. He shot the two deputies who were guarding him, leaped on a horse, and rode off.

"That's him!"

Pat Garrett was soon back on the Kid's trail. Knowing the places they used to go as friends, the sheriff guessed correctly that the Kid would head toward the hideout of a friend, Pete Maxwell. Garrett and his posse sneaked up on the place in the middle of the night.

The Kid, who was awake, called to Maxwell because he noticed some strange figures on the porch. A reply came back: "That's him!" and Garrett shot the Kid just above the heart, killing him instantly.

Billy the Kid was shot just above the heart by his friend-turned-sheriff, Pat Garrett.

BONNIE AND CLYDE

Clyde Barrow 1909–1934
Bonnie Parker 1910–1934

During the Depression of the 1930s, a crime wave swept across America. Among the gangsters responsible for the violence was the young couple Bonnie and Clyde.

Clyde Barrow was born on March 24, 1909. He began to steal when he was 15. Clyde came from a poor background and had a difficult childhood. One of his few pleasures was watching cowboy films at the movies. He imagined himself to be like the outlaw Jesse James.

Bonnie Parker was born on October 1, 1910, in Texas, and grew up in Cement City, a tough, run-down area. Bonnie was an intelligent and loving child who adored her mother. But she was also known for her sudden, violent outbursts and her cravings for attention.

Love at first sight

Bonnie and Clyde met in January 1930 and were instantly attracted to each other. They soon fell in love. Bonnie was overcome with grief when Clyde was imprisoned for burglary and car theft. She smuggled a gun into jail, and with it Clyde managed to escape.

Bonnie Parker and Clyde Barrow first met in January 1930. They soon became two of the most ruthless gangsters in America.

The Great Depression

There were many different reasons for the Great Depression of 1929 to 1940, which had far-reaching effects worldwide. In the United States nearly 14 million people, or about one in four, were unemployed, and thousands of businesses went bankrupt. Also, in some areas, the land had been **overcropped** and had turned to dust. There was no **welfare system** for those who had fallen on hard times. Some turned to crime to make ends meet.

A long prison sentence

A few days later, Clyde was arrested again, this time for robbing a railroad-ticket office at gunpoint. He was sentenced to 14 years imprisonment in a grim Texas prison that was known to be very tough. Not even Bonnie could get him out of this prison, so Clyde came up with his own gruesome plan. He persuaded another prisoner to cut off two of his toes with an ax, hoping the prison authorities would feel sorry for him and let him go. Clyde didn't know that he was already being considered for **parole** and was eventually released.

Life on the road

Once he was out of jail, Clyde rejoined Bonnie. They stole a car, teamed up with three others, and decided to head for west Dallas. The newly formed gang drove for hundreds of miles, stealing one car after another. They often lived in the car for long periods at a time. Over the next few years, Bonnie and Clyde and their gang robbed many banks, restaurants, and filling stations, but their biggest haul was only $3,500. During these years they killed 12 people, and they became known as one of the most daring and violent gangs of the era.

Unemployed men wait in line for food in New York, during the Great Depression in the 1930s.

Public Enemy Number One

In 1933 Bonnie and Clyde decided to hide out in Missouri. They were joined by Clyde's brother, Buck, and his wife, Blanche. They rented a house and led a quiet life for a couple of weeks, until the neighbors became suspicious and informed the police.

The house was surrounded, and a shoot-out followed, which left two police officers dead and Clyde slightly injured. The gang escaped, and the authorities put every available person on the job of capturing Bonnie and Clyde, dead or alive. Clyde was given the title Public Enemy Number One of the southwest. They were chased around the country as they continued to commit crime after crime.

A bloody attack

In February 1934 the chase ended when the gang was again surrounded in Missouri by the police. Bonnie and Clyde managed to escape, following a fierce gunfight, but this time the police caused serious casualties. Buck was riddled with bullets and died in a hospital six days later. Blanche, who had been shot and blinded, decided to stay with her husband. She was eventually charged and sent to trial and was sentenced to ten years in prison.

Bonnie and Clyde photographed each other while on the run from the law.

Clyde was declared Public Enemy Number One of the southwest in 1933.

Pretty Boy Floyd

Pretty Boy Floyd (1901–1934), was a tall, handsome laborer from Oklahoma, who turned to crime during the Great Depression. Floyd robbed banks and shot anybody who got in his way. It is said that he killed ten people. He was gunned down by the **FBI** in Ohio. Like Bonnie and Clyde, Floyd became a legend. Once, when he was on the run, he was fed by a poor farming family. When he left, the farmer's wife found a thousand-dollar bill under Floyd's empty plate.

Fatal ambush

Bonnie and Clyde stayed on the run for the next three months. A lawman named Frank Hamer trailed them across nine states. On May 23, 1934, acting on some information from a former gang member, Hamer and five other lawmen set up an ambush outside Arcadia, Louisiana.

Riddled with bullets

Bonnie and Clyde were killed as the Ford V8 they were driving was riddled with bullets from nearly one hundred rounds of ammunition. Their bodies were put on display in a local furniture shop. Thousands of people went to see the corpses of the most famous gangster couple in history.

The bullet-riddled Ford Sedan car in which Bonnie and Clyde died is on exhibit in Las Vegas, Nevada.

GLOSSARY

Alias A made-up name used by criminals and other outlaws when they want to keep their identity a secret.

Allegiance A person's loyalty to a king, a queen, or a country.

Ambush A surprise attack from a concealed place.

Ammunition Bullets and cannonballs that are fired from guns and cannons.

Assassin Someone who commits murder.

Blockade To cut off a place by surrounding it with ships or troops.

Bootlegging Making and selling something illegally.

Bow The front part of a ship.

Brand The owner's mark on cattle.

Canton A political division of Switzerland.

Civil War A war between people of the same country. The Civil War was fought between the northern and southern states of the U.S. The southern states wanted to keep slavery and thought they should have more power to govern themselves. The northern states wanted to ban slavery and felt the president and Congress should rule the whole country equally.

Confederation A collection of states united into one area or country.

Cutlass A broad, curved sword with a short handle.

Exile To force a person to leave his or her home or country.

FBI Federal Bureau of Investigation, part of the Justice Department in the United States.

Footboy A boy servant.

Foot regiment A group of soldiers that travels on foot rather than by ship or horse.

Fortress A large castle, well protected from enemies.

Frigate A medium-sized warship.

Gallows A place selected for hangings.

Governor A person sent to organize and rule a country in place of the king or queen.

Guerrilla A fighter who wages war by ambush and surprise attack.

HMS His or Her Majesty's Ship.

Homestead A small house and plot of land.

Immigrants People who are arriving in a new country to live.

Jacobites The supporters of James II of England after his removal from the throne in 1688.

King's flag The flag of a ruling king or queen, under which a ship sails.

Legend A very old story passed down from generation to generation that may or may not be true.

Medieval The period of history between A.D. 1100 and A.D. 1500. It is also called the Middle Ages.

Native Americans The original inhabitants of America before Europeans arrived.

Overcropped Land that has been exhausted by growing crops continuously.

Pardon To forgive or excuse a person for a crime by not punishing them.

Parole When a prisoner is released from jail before his or her prison sentence is finished, usually for good behavior.

Peasant A farmworker who usually earns very little money.

Plunder To steal valuable goods by force.

Posse A group of people who ride out with the sheriff or another lawman to search for outlaws.

Priory The name of a building where nuns or monks live.

Privateer A sailor on a privately owned ship used by a government to attack enemy ships in times of war.

Red Cross The international organization that provides medical care for victims of war and natural disasters.

Resistance A group of people who fight against an enemy force in their country.

Rustling Stealing horses and cattle.

Seal A ring decorated with the badge or emblem of the king or a noble.

Spanish Succession The war fought between 1701–1713 by the major European countries for control of Spain and its empire.

Tenant A peasant farmer who leased farmland from a landowner. In return, the tenant would work for the landlord and fight for him in times of war.

Traitor A person who betrays his or her country.

Welfare system A system set up by the government to help people who have fallen on hard times.

INDEX